Wombat's Burrow

by Dee Phillips

Consultants:

Stella Reid
Wildhaven Wildlife Shelter, St. Andrews, Victoria, Australia

Kimberly Brenneman, PhD
National Institute for Early Education Research, Rutgers University, New Brunswick, New Jersey

BEARPORT
PUBLISHING

New York, New York

Credits
Cover, © Jurgen & Christine Sohns/FLPA and public domain; 2–3, © Pete Oxford/Minden Pictures/FLPA; 4, © Jess Fallon; 5, © Gerry Pearce/Alamy; 7TL, © Jurgen & Christine Sohns/FLPA; 7TR, © Brent Hedges/Nature Picture Library; 7B, © Marco Tomasini/Shutterstock; 8, © Cyril Ruoso/Minden Pictures/FLPA; 9, © St. John Pound/Alamy; 10, © Patricio Robles Gil/Nature Picture Library; 11, © Marco Tomasini/Shutterstock; 12, © Mitch Reardon/Science Photo Library; 13, © FiledIMAGE/Shutterstock; 14, © Caleb Elrea/Australis Wild; 15, © John Carnemolla/Shutterstock; 16, © Jurgen & Christine Sohns/FLPA; 17, © Gerhard Koertner/Photoshot; 18–19, © Pete Oxford/Minden Pictures/FLPA; 20, © Dave Watts/Alamy; 21, © Andrew Forsyth/FLPA; 22TL, © Rob Walls/Alamy; 22R, © Marco Tomasini/Shutterstock and © iStockphoto/Thinkstock; 23TL, © Jess Fallon; 23TC, © Marco Tomasini/Shutterstock; 23TR, © Gerhard Koertner/Photoshot; 23BL, © Jurgen & Christine Sohns/FLPA; 23BC, © yotrak/Shutterstock; 23BR, © Pete Oxford/Minden Pictures/FLPA.

Publisher: Kenn Goin
Senior Editor: Joyce Tavolacci
Creative Director: Spencer Brinker
Design: Emma Randall
Editor: Mark J. Sachner
Photo Researcher: Ruby Tuesday Books Ltd

Library of Congress Cataloging-in-Publication Data

Phillips, Dee, 1967– author.
  Wombat's burrow / by Dee Phillips.
      pages cm. — (The hole truth! : underground animal life)
  Includes bibliographical references and index.
  ISBN 978-1-62724-091-8 (library binding) — ISBN 1-62724-091-8 (library binding)
  1. Wombats—Behavior—Juvenile literature. 2. Wombats—Habitat—Juvenile literature. I. Title.
II. Series: Phillips, Dee, 1967– Hole truth!
  QL737.M39P49 2014
  599.2'4—dc23
                                    2013036884

For more information, write to Bearport Publishing Company, Inc., 45 West 21st Street, Suite 3B, New York, New York 10010. Printed in the United States of America.

10 9 8 7 6 5 4 3 2 1

Contents

Welcome to a Wombat's Home

It's a warm summer evening.

Hidden in some tall grass is an entrance hole to a **burrow**.

Suddenly, a large, hairy face peeks out of the hole.

It's a wombat that has been sleeping all day.

As night falls, the hungry animal leaves its underground home to search for food.

entrance hole to a burrow

wombat

A wombat spends more than half of every day sleeping in its burrow.

All About Wombats

Wombats are strong, medium-sized animals that look like little bears.

An adult wombat is about three feet (1 m) long.

Wombats live in Australia.

They dig their burrows in grassy areas.

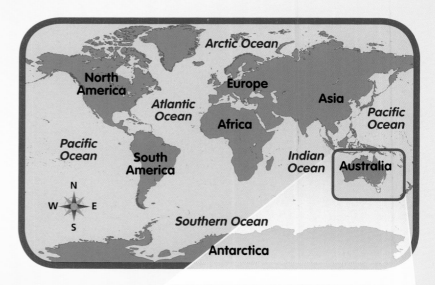

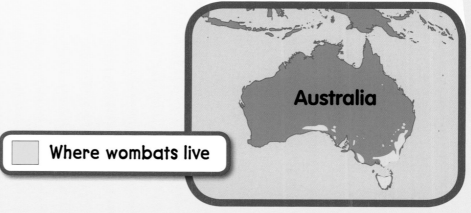

Where wombats live

There are three kinds of wombats. They are the common wombat, the southern hairy-nosed wombat, and the northern hairy-nosed wombat.

southern hairy-nosed wombat

northern hairy-nosed wombat

common wombat

Describe what a wombat looks like to someone who has never seen one before.

Built for Digging

Wombats are powerful diggers.

Their strong shoulders, large paws, and long claws help them build their burrows.

First, the animal digs an entrance hole with its front paws.

It pushes the loose soil out of the hole with its back feet.

Then, using its front paws, the wombat digs a long, main tunnel.

claws

A wombat lives in an area called a **home range**. A common wombat may dig up to 12 burrows in its home range.

Try to imagine what the inside of a wombat's burrow looks like. How long do you think the tunnel might be? Do you think the burrow has rooms?

a wombat digging

A Wombat's Burrow

The main tunnel in a wombat's burrow can be up to 100 feet (30.5 m) long.

A wombat digs shorter tunnels that are connected to the main one.

At the end of some of the tunnels, a wombat digs rooms.

It uses these underground rooms for sleeping.

a sleeping wombat

Day and Night

The places where wombats live can be very hot in the daytime.

So wombats spend the day resting underground, where it's cool.

When evening comes, the animals leave their burrows to find food.

Wombats eat grass, leaves, tree bark, and **moss**.

In the morning, wombats return to one of their burrows to sleep.

a wombat leaving its burrow at night

a wombat eating grass

A wombat may walk for more than one mile (1.6 km) each night looking for food.

Some animals try to attack and eat wombats. How do you think wombats stay safe from these enemies?

Escaping from Enemies

Animals such as foxes and wild dogs called dingoes hunt and eat wombats.

To escape from these enemies, a wombat dives into its burrow.

Then it blocks the entrance with its hard, bony bottom.

The wombat's behind is so tough that attackers can't bite through it!

hard, bony backside

a wombat diving into its burrow

When a wombat is blocking its tunnel, an enemy may squeeze onto the wombat's back. Then the wombat uses its body to crush the enemy against the burrow's roof.

dingo

Female wombats use their burrows for something other than resting and staying safe. What do you think they do inside their burrows?

Baby Wombats

Wombats usually live alone.

However, males and females come together to **mate**.

About one month later, a female gives birth to a baby in her burrow.

The tiny baby is called a joey and is about the size of a jellybean.

The joey climbs into a **pouch** on its mother's belly.

Inside the pouch, it drinks milk from her body.

a male and female wombat

a joey in its mother's pouch

A newborn wombat has no hair. The tiny baby cannot see or hear because its eyes and ears are not fully grown yet.

A Joey's Life

A joey lives in its mother's pouch for up to eight months.

During this time, the joey's eyes and ears develop and its hair grows.

As the little wombat drinks its mother's milk, it grows bigger and bigger.

Finally, the joey is ready to leave the pouch.

Wombats belong to a group of animals called **marsupials**. All marsupials give birth to tiny babies that are not fully formed. A baby marsupial finishes growing inside its mother's pouch, instead of inside her body.

All Grown Up

Once a wombat leaves its mother's pouch, it begins to eat plants.

As the joey gets bigger and stronger, it practices digging tunnels.

Then, at about 18 months old, the joey is ready to leave its mother.

At first, it might live alone in one of its mother's burrows.

Soon, however, the young wombat will dig an underground home all for itself!

five-month-old joey

mother wombat

Wombats can live for about 10 to 15 years in the wild. Wombats in zoos have lived for more than 30 years.

ten-month-old joey

Science Lab

Wombats leave piles of block-shaped poop, or scat, outside their burrows and around their home range. This tells other wombats who the home range belongs to.

wombat scat

Be a Wombat Scientist

Imagine you are a scientist who studies wombats. You can find out what a wombat has been doing by looking for its scat. Look at the map and try answering these questions:

1) Which of its burrows did the wombat recently visit? How can you tell?

2) Do you think the wombat has been eating at the north grassland or the south grassland? Why do you think so?

3) Why do you think the wombat left scat beside the fallen tree?

(The answers are on page 24.)

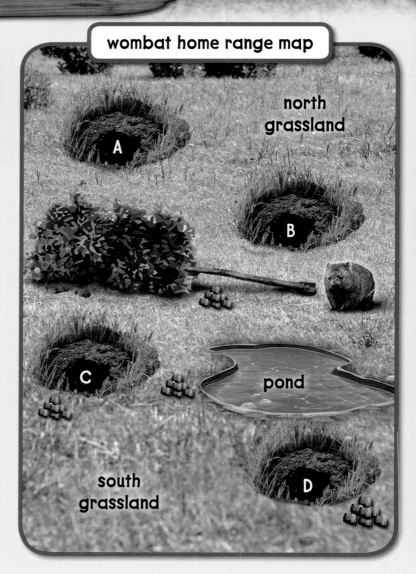

wombat home range map

north grassland

A

B

C

pond

south grassland

D

Science Words

burrow (BUR-oh) an entrance hole and tunnels dug by an animal to live in

home range (HOHM RAYNJ) the area where an animal lives and finds its food

marsupials (mar-SOO-pee-uhlz) a group of animals in which the young are raised in pouches on their mothers' bellies

mate (MAYT) to come together in order to have young

moss (MAWSS) a fuzzy plant that sometimes covers rocks or trees

pouch (POUCH) a pocket-like part of a marsupial's belly used for carrying her young

Index

Read More

Gates, Margo. *Wombats (Blastoff! Readers: Animal Safari)*. Minneapolis, MN: Bellwether Media (2014).

George, Lynn. *Wombats: Burrow Builders (Animal Architects)*. New York: Power Kids Press (2011).

Learn More Online

To learn more about wombats, visit **www.bearportpublishing.com/ TheHoleTruth!**

About the Author

Dee Phillips lives near the ocean on the southwest coast of England. She develops and writes nonfiction and fiction books for children of all ages.

Answer for Page 18

Kangaroos, wallabies, koalas, Tasmanian devils, and opossums are all marsupials.

kangaroo

Tasmanian devil

Answers for Page 22

1) The wombat visited burrows C and D. You can tell because it left scat nearby.

2) The wombat has probably been eating at the south grassland because it visited nearby burrows.

3) The wombat may want to dig a burrow under the fallen tree or eat the tree's leaves. It may have left scat by the tree to tell other wombats to stay out of its home range.